Chief and Riley

Andrea and Riley Shales

Illustrated by
Dwain Esper

AuthorHouse™
1663 Liberty Drive
Bloomington, IN 47403
www.authorhouse.com
Phone: 1 (800) 839–8640

Published by AuthorHouse 02/13/2015

ISBN: 978–1–4918–7097–6 (sc)
ISBN: 978–1–4918–7098–3 (e)

Library of Congress Control Number: 2015900940

Print information available on the last page.

authorHOUSE®

Chief and Riley

Riley is an adventurous boy who likes to climb trees, explore the woods, ride his bike, and play in the park. He lives with his mom, his dad, and two solid black Pomeranians. Whenever Riley has a hamburger, he always saves the last few bites for the two dogs because it's their favorite treat. Even so, the dogs seem to prefer his mom (they follow her everywhere!), and since the dogs are getting older and don't have much energy, they aren't too interested in playing with Riley.

Riley asked his mom and dad for a dog of his own. "Please, can I get my very own dog?" Riley begged.

Since the family already had two Pomeranians, adding another dog could be disastrous, his mom explained. Taking care of even just one dog was a lot of work. Taking care of two dogs was even more work. But taking care of three dogs? That was a ton of work!

"Please, Mama! Please, Daddy! I will take care of him. Please!" Riley said.

After a long discussion, Riley's parents decided that it could work if the whole family shared the responsibilities of taking the dogs out, feeding them, washing them, walking them, and playing with them. Riley decided that one of his jobs would be to help the new puppy stay in shape by swimming with him, running, playing, and walking.

The next day, the family headed out to find a dog for Riley. They visited several different dog breeders, including German shepherds and Dobermans. Riley held several puppies, but none of the dogs seemed to bond with Riley. Riley's mom wondered, Will we ever find the right dog?

The next facility had twelve German shepherd puppies. Riley sat on the beautiful green grass and exclaimed, "This is him! This is my dog. I love him!"

Riley's parents turned around to see the puppy jumping out of the blue kiddie pool onto Riley's lap. He began licking Riley's face.

Riley's mom and dad said, "Looks like that dog picked you! He already loves you."

As soon as Riley attached the leash to the collar, the puppy playfully tugged at the leash with his mouth. Then, as Riley began walking him around, the energetic puppy put a bounce to his step. They were already buddies, and that special bond had already started to develop between Riley and his dog.

The puppy needed a name. The breeder said that the puppy was from an O litter, so he needed a name that began with the letter O. He explained to Riley that when purebred breeders have litters, they name the litter with the corresponding letter of the alphabet. This was this breeder's fifteenth litter, and since fifteenth letter of the alphabet is O, the puppy needed to be registered with a name that started with O. "It helps trace a dog's bloodlines, and it's considered the legal name," the breeder explained. Then he said to Riley, "You can always pick a different 'house' name for the dog if you want to."

Riley's mom wanted to name him Oprah.

"No. I think that's a girl's name," Riley said.

"What about Oscar?" Riley's dad suggested.

"No. I like Chief," Riley said. "He looks like a chief to me. He stands strong and is always looking back and forth and all over the area, like he's in charge."

Riley's dad said, "I think he looks like a chief too, but Chief doesn't start with an O!"

Riley's mom had a suggestion. "Let's look up names up on the computer," she said.

They found a website that sectioned names off by letter. They checked the O names. Riley spotted the name Chief right away. He pointed to the computer, and the whole family read aloud, "Okemos." They learned that Okemos had its origins in the Native American Ojibwa language, and it was a name meaning "a little chief." It was perfect!

Chief and Riley did everything together. They were inseparable. They took naps outside in the hammock, they played tag, and one of the funniest things to watch them play was hide—and—seek. They played for hours trying to find each other.

One day, Riley was hiding in his bedroom under his bed. Chief crouched down, rested his head on the floor with his tail wagging wildly, and appeared to be smiling as he looked under the bed and found Riley.

Riley tilted his head back and burst out laughing. "You found me! Good boy. Good find."

Riley loved to play sports. From football to hockey to swimming, Chief played them all with Riley! Chief seemed to understand how to play all the different sports. If Riley had the ball, Chief knew that he had to get it and run away. Chief was a very large and active dog, and he seemed liked a brother to Riley.

One day, Riley's family decided to move. Riley was sad. He didn't want to leave his house, his room, or his yard.

Riley confided in Chief. Chief was his best friend and a good listener. Riley looked at Chief and said, "Buddy, I'm scared to move."

Riley worried that things would not be the same. What would their house be like? Where would they play? He told Chief that he did not want to move. As Riley told Chief about his concerns, Chief laid his head on Riley's lap. Chief had a way of making Riley understand that he was not alone. They sat together in silence.

"Moving is a very difficult thing," Riley's mom said. "Riley and Chief, we understand how you feel, and it's okay to be scared. We understand that you may feel anxious. Do you have any questions?"

Riley nodded and said, "Will our new house have a pool? Will we be able to swim? And play outside? What if I don't like our new house?"

Riley's mom said, "I'm sure you'll love our new house and new neighborhood. You can ride your bike and play basketball, football, and hockey. We don't have a pool right now, but we'll be sure to get one!"

Chief responded by smiling at Riley's mom.

Riley petted Chief's head and said, "Okay."

"Well," Riley's mom said, "if you think of anything else, please ask me. I do know this: you will love our new home. The backyard is full of beautiful trees. Good things will come from this move! You'll have more grand adventures in our new home! This will be better for the entire family! Do you want to go see our new house?"

"Yes!" shouted Riley. Chief jumped off the bed.

The family went on a forty—five—minute drive to their new home. It was as beautiful as Riley's mom had explained. The house was at the end of a street, and a forest full of trees surrounded the home. Riley jumped out of the car, holding his football. He walked down the driveway and spotted a hill that would be perfect to ride his bike down.

"Let's go in!" Riley's dad said.

As the family walked into their new home, Riley and Chief looked at each other.   Riley said to Chief, "Buddy, this is our new home. Let's go exploring!"

The next adventure of Chief and Riley had begun.

CPSIA information can be obtained at www.ICGtesting.com
Printed in the USA
LVOW02s2242150415

434674LV00026B/174/P